# SO YOU WANT A's IN COLLEGE?

## Winning the Professor and Beating Your Competition: A Handbook

## Tommy S. Horne

# PREFACE

If you are looking for standard advice on academic success, then this book is not for you. If you are looking for instruction on how to secure the A grade, then this book is for you. This book is different than others of its kind because it offers insight into real strategy as opposed to lofty advice on good study habits.

This book shows how to win the professor and make A grades through the use of interpersonal influence based on political and military theory. This knowledge has been attained by the author's documented and practical experience in politics and the military. It teaches the application of these theories in the college setting. This approach instructs students on changing the odds of academic success in their favor in a real way.

This handbook was written for students who want to have a hand in designing their futures. There are many books published by honor societies and learning institutions on how to be academically successful. Most of these publications, CDs, and products focus on old themes of note taking, listening, and other traditional skills. The strategies in this book should be understood as guiding principles and not a list of rules. In *The Art of War,* Sun Tzu demonstrated this principle by writing, "Therefore, just as water retains no constant shape, so in warfare there are no constant conditions." Keep the basic principles in mind as you discover which tactics work for you and the given situation in your academic study.

# ABOUT THE AUTHOR

Tommy S. Horne served as an officer in the United States Army. He is a veteran of Operation Enduring Freedom. He is a published author and photographer in an army-wide professional journal. During college, he served as a campaign manager of a successful state district political race and an assistant campaign manager of another local county election. He was a high-honors graduate in college and earned a bachelor of arts in political science. He belongs to numerous honors associations.

# ACKNOWLEDGEMENTS

This book is dedicated to all of my teachers.

# TABLE OF CONTENTS

# CHAPTER 1

# RECOGNIZING PERSONAL OBJECTIVES AND GOALS

**"It is not the critic who counts: not the man who points out how the strong man stumbles or where the doer of deeds could have done better. The credit belongs to the man who is actually in the arena [...], so that his place shall never be with those cold and timid souls who knew neither victory nor defeat."**

**-Theodore Roosevelt**

Know yourself and know your goals before ever even applying to college. The following information is fundamental. It would be instructive to consider these points before moving on to actual tactics. These points are on developing goals, having high school experience, and building on past success. This is not a motivational book, for that is another thing entirely. However, before you begin to learn tactics, you must learn about yourself. Sun Tzu wrote, "If you know yourself but not the enemy, for every victory gained, you will also suffer a defeat."

## Develop Goals

Develop goals. Goals are to be developed and then constantly cultivated. They keep you focused, and you must remain flexible if they do not work out exactly as planned. I have kept this at the forefront of my mind as a lifelong martial artist.

I began learning the importance of goals at a young age. I began studying martial arts at age seven and began learning about goals almost immediately from our instructor, Master David Carr. He always instructed us that the journey through martial arts is much like a mountain climber at the base of the mountain. You realize that you are an overwhelmingly long way from the top.

The point of Master Carr's lesson was that you will reach each level (belt) and should keep climbing. Standing at the base and looking up will be discouraging and challenging. There will be distractions along the way. These jagged and slippery edges are to be improvised for.

Eventually, a person will reach the top of the mountain through perseverance. Once a black belt, he would realize that his journey had just begun and that he had only learned the basics.

I became a black belt at fifteen. I always remembered this lesson. I saw hundreds of students come in and out of the martial arts class over the years. In many ways seeing others fall out emboldened me and encouraged me to see this lifelong dream through.

Develop your goals by starting with broad concepts. Ask yourself, what are my goals? Do they include wealth, prestige, power, family, or happiness? A command staff section will have a conference before planning any military operation. Basic end states are discussed. The staff subsequently clears the information and breaks the broad concepts into a very detailed plan.

The broad ideas allow you to begin to refine your goals. Too many students enter college without much of an end state in mind. However, most people have a general clue as to where they want to be in twenty years or so. Nobody wants to be poor, alone, or dependent. There are not many people who *planned* on these things to happen to them.

Conversely, how many self-made millionaires did not plan on being a millionaire? Did it just happen through a fluke or lottery? The answer is assuredly NO. First, these people started small, saving and spending less than they earned. Eventually, they moved to investments. Finally, they took calculated risks in order to secure a viable business for themselves.

The self-made millionaire at age eighteen or twenty-five would not be able to prophesy what specific business he would own in thirty years. However, he would be able to tell you about his current savings and investment plan.

I have been encouraged to plan, prepare, plan again, and prepare some more throughout my military experience. This is the essential function of military officers at all echelons of command. Not all plans work, but you have additional courses of action already prepared.

Take this idea of planning and run with it. Tailor it to suit your circumstances. The following is a good technique to begin your life planning. First decide where you see yourself in twenty years. Then ask, "How will I get to that point?" Then ask the question, "How will I get there?" at least five more times. Eventually you will get close to the position you are at now. At the very least, you will have put some serious and deliberate thought into your future.

## Self-Reflection

Self-reflection is invaluable. Devote time to thinking about your own abilities, propensities, and aptitudes. Only honest assessments will help you.

Before we go further, let us take a mental assessment and consider a few questions. Who am I mentally? Who am I spiritually? Who are my mentors? Who discourages me? Where is my life headed? What kind of life do I want? Where will I be when I am sixty-five? Am I interested in security or wealth? What do I fear most? What have I done to influence where I am now? These questions are important. Take some time to think about these. Really think about them and reflect. Just thinking in depth about these questions will put you ahead of other students starting out in college.

## Non-High School Honor Students

Your ability to succeed in college will not be based on your success or failure in high school. College is a new beast and calls for a whole new strategy. Some high schools attempt to emulate the college setting. These try to model class discussions and formats after college as well. They do this out of good intentions.

High school and college are based on entirely different organizations. The former is based on a rigid and compressed system. There are specifically marked times for class, clearly established standards, and lists and lists of rules to follow. The subject matter taught is seldom disputed, if at all.

College is organized much more loosely than high school. Class attendance is negotiable and not standardized. Class standards are at the pleasure of each professor. The class material is fluid and constantly being added to in respective professional fields.

Essentially, your professors will be a lot different than your high school teachers. The class organization, the standards, and almost everything else will be entirely new to you. The university is going to be categorically different than the schoolhouse.

View college as an opportunity to start over. Remember that after college, no one (including graduate schools and employers) is concerned with minor scholastic achievements from high school. This is said at risk of brashness, but it is important to toss this notion aside.

There have been countless high school honor students who failed out of college. It would be impossible to accurately recall how many of these cases I ran into when I was in the army and throughout college. These were often smart people. They came from great homes. They were gifted high school students but lost focus and gave up in the wake of the challenges that college brings to bear.

Seeking out this book out attests to your willingness to not fall into the fray. You will develop a sound plan to attain and maintain success in college.

It would be instructive here to make a historical point. Niccolo Machiavelli's age was much more politically unstable than ours today. In his day, parts of Europe were still divided into small republics. Princes and rulers of each republic would vie for more power through usurping other small city-states. He wrote *The Prince* as a gift to his ruler and as an instruction manual on statecraft.

In *The Prince* Machiavelli modeled two different types of rulers. The first were those who came to power through fortune. This was usually in the form of inheritance. The second were those leaders who came to power through prowess. This was usually in the form of force of arms.

The ruler who comes to power through good fortune, Niccolo describes, needs to rely less on his fortune thus making his rule far more consequential. Everything the ruler does outside of simply inheriting a republic will make him more convincing as a leader to other states, his people, and his inner court. Niccolo writes that the ruler who comes to power through prowess attains his power with more difficulty but once attained, holds power with ease.

This ancient wisdom is still useful today. View high school honor students as those who came to academic power through fortune. These students are sometimes gifted but also sometimes the products of a lax grading system and academic structure. If someone excels in a lax school environment, they may have unrealistic expectations about themselves. Others, seeing that success, will also be affected negatively. They will put their self-worth at risk. Conclusively, both of groups of students believe in a sort of illusion. You, however, will not rest on your laurels from high school nor will you allow others' accomplishments (sometimes artificial) to affect you negatively.

Success tends to make people lazy. There is a good chance for complacency to set in once you have gotten used to success. There is always a lingering temptation to rest on your laurels. Prepare for the next four-year battle that looms near. Unless you are naturally born for academic study, it will be an extra challenge to remain hungry.

I will never forget the words of my lineman coach. He would say, "Stay hungry!" and "Leave it all out on the field." The pitch of emotions during a close-and-hard-fought game at half time is feverish. You experience pride, desperation, sadness, and excitement all at once. You go into the locker room with bruises and rips in your jersey and sometimes with blood on your knuckles.

Our team had not been to the state championship in over ten years. During this account, the fever pitch of emotions was at an all-time high, and this game was our chance to go to the playoff.

When Coach McQuin told us those words, we were inspired. I still hear those words in my mind. I heard them in college when I wanted to quit. I heard them when I was nervous about asking a girl on a date. I heard them in Afghanistan as a platoon leader.

You have to stay hungry the entire game. Never quit. Never give up. You must leave it all out there on the field. This means giving it all you have in your hunger and leaving the field without the looming doubts of, "Could I have done more?"

If you were successful in high school, then you must consider two things. First, how substantial were your accomplishments actually? You will likely discover this from the self-reflection portion earlier in this chapter.

Second, you must consider how willing you are to stay hungry, to stay the course, and to leave it all out there on the field. You must harness this individually and earnestly. Not everyone will be able to. You, however, will adapt and overcome.

If you were not academically successful in high school, view this as an advantage! You, like the second group of Machiavelli's leaders, will have to come to power through force. You will ensure your tenure in academic success like the rulers who came to power through fortune needed to make their rule more convincing. You will have to overcome the low expectations that others (including possibly yourself) that others have placed on you during high school or secondary school.

Some high school teachers have a proclivity to gravitate around the smarter students in class. It is much easier to teach those who are making good grades than those who are struggling. This is a weakness in human nature. It is an expression of people's natural tendency to go to the path of least resistance. Granted, there are those students who deserve no attention as they intentionally disrupt learning or do not care whatsoever. These are not the students I am talking about here.

The students I am describing and writing to are those normal students who make normal grades. These students did not receive coddling or special attention from teachers and thus were not made to believe that they were special or were high achievers. This potentially destructive arrangement breeds artificial expectations in both the honor students and the normal students.

Consider those times you may have been cast aside, weren't called on, or did not receive those favorable glances from the teachers like the honor students did. Use these memories and channel them to your advantage. When you enter college, you are on an even playing field. Self-discipline rules the day. You and the honor student will make daily choices that will have long-range consequences. Some of these will include staying up late and studying, actually attending class, preparing in advance for assignments, and managing an even class load. These core decisions are not based on any type of academic prowess but are simply choices made through self-discipline and proper planning.

I was always an average student from kindergarten to senior year at the same school. I largely went to this school with the same group of colleagues. The school is highly regarded for academic excellence in the area. The same kids who became academic giants in elementary stayed that way through middle school and high school. College changed everything for many of them. Many began to fall away immediately into the fray of alcoholism, party life, and the general rigors of adjusting to independence. To be certain, some of my colleagues who were always star students are still star students, as they excel in advanced degrees. However, many of them have left and reentered college several times as they found the adjustment to be very difficult.

On the other hand, I was a straight-C student from kindergarten to twelfth grade. I always knew that I had a lot of potential. However, I never could excel in such a rigid system as found in the standard high school format.

However, I've always been driven. I knew from an early age what it means to persue your own destiny. I graduated college with high honors and a 3.85 GPA. I achieved this through the tactics and perspectives that I will outline in the following chapters.

## High School Honor Students

Prepare for the next battle. Disregard any notions that college will be a continuance of the parade. You are now dealing with college professors and the college environment. The organizational cultures of high school and college are completely different. The time of strictly mandated assignments and a teacher closely watching your progress is over. If you were a top student in high school, then build on it! Take the confidence you learned from high school and build on it. It will be a challenge to stay hungry, but it is altogether possible and likely. Always build and adapt; never remain stagnant.

The greatest asset to being a high school honor student is that it demonstrates a proclivity for academic success. The most important thing to do is never allow complacency or burnout to creep in and destroy the progress you have made. You are now in the arena where it counts, so fight hard and play for keeps.

## Developing Goals

Once you have realized your potential, develop specific goals. For instance, if your goal is to be wealthy, you have only gone half way. Once you have specified your goals, begin to think about the most practical and sure-fire ways of attaining them.

Keep it simple. Simplicity is one the US Army's nine principles of war. If a plan is too intricate or contains too many moving parts, it should be refined. Put the highest emphasis on your goals. Take care of the matter at hand but always focus on your goals.

Many times when young adults are asked about future goals, they give general answers. This is because most people never actually take the time and commitment to sit down and hammer out a good plan. Developing an attainable goal requires three things. First, give yourself an honest evaluation through self-reflection. Second, write down a tentative strategy chronicling your beginning of college, to your first interview, and all the way to retirement. Finally, tell other people about your goals.

## Self-Assessment Deriving from Yourself Alone. Jealous Loved Ones?

Honesty is the key to self-assessment. Have you ever actually devoted any time to understanding your own weaknesses or strengths? This does not mean going off other people's assessments of you. This bears repeating: please do not assess yourself based on other people's observations. Other people have their own complete set of motives. When you speak to someone, you actually are dealing with the full gamut of his or her hidden insecurities. Be it a survival instinct, or whatever it may be, some people will discourage you and not give you an honest assessment of you. No one wants to be "left in the dust" of success. Most people are not vindictive or actually aim to do you harm. However, they just will not be conducive to your success or really be your advocate.

There actually are sinister people who flagrantly discourage you or insult you. The best way to deal with these people is simple. STAY AWAY FROM THEM AT ALL COSTS. This is verbatim advice I received from my sociology professor in college. This was a key take-away I have always remembered from the class years ago.

Thomas Edison was a businessman before he was a scientist. This is a little known fact and accepted from most historical perspectives. He would steal technology from his underlings and then run to get a patent for the invention in order to make a profit. He was also recorded as stiffing individuals on payments. This is important to know so that you understand that academics are people too. They are not noble by the sole virtue of their tenured chair. Always be aware of others, sometimes even your teachers.

The Thomas Edisons of this day are lying in wait. I recently had lunch with a lifelong friend. We will call him Matt. Matt is a brilliant graduate student of engineering. He told me about a few ideas he has had to patent. He has endured being ostracized by jealous fellow students ever since expressing these ideas openly. His professor presented the same idea for this technology as his own in a presentation. The professor did this within the week of Matt expressing his ideas. As soon as the professor presented it, he immediately left the room. Eerie. Matt is currently seeking a patent for his prospectively very lucrative idea before someone else reaps the reward.

Matt was confused and alarmed by this peculiar behavior. I told Matt that this is not bizarre at all. In fact, this reaction from fellow students and the actions of his professor are very predictable. These students are small minded and have deep-seated reservations about those with imagination. Imagination upsets the herd and altogether encourages these people to group together in a faction to exclude the visionary.

This kind of professor is a wolf lying in wait. As she encourages her students to discuss their plans with her under the guise of development and instruction, she actually is scanning and waiting to rob the students. This is not a book about the depravity of man and the unending discussions on that issue. I will leave that to the philosophical. This is a real-life account that is personal to me as it involves a close friend of mine and vividly illustrates this section's thesis. It should also be noted that this kind of professor is not the norm but definitely a kind to watch for. Fortunately, all of my professors have been invaluable and cherished mentors.

Do not have any contact with these cold and lonely souls. Even people who follow up an insult with a "just kidding" attitude deserve no attention. These cowards are toxic and should be treated as such. Because they have realized their prospects and dreams are flattened, they are out to prove the world is flat is well. Simply cut these insidious urchins out of your life. If you must deal with them—say you work with them—do not give in. Stay constantly vigilant in protecting your dignity. Be stern. Be confident. Be assertive. Never be afraid to look them in the eye.

Even people who love you will sometimes not give you an honest judgment of you. They may want to appease you or encourage you. From this they may inflate your actual abilities and strengths. Although someone may love you, he or she may be harboring his or her own full range of insecurities. They are just as susceptible to jealousy or vindictiveness as your friends may be. Stay vigilant and aware. Analyze everyone's motives.

## The Value of a Trusted Mentor

Hold on to those cherished people who give you an honest view of yourself. Cherish their time and be patient with the advice they dispense. Enlist them as mentors and constant companions. A person like this is not someone who will hold your hand and tell you everything's going to be all right. It is someone who has your future in mind and is not afraid to correct you or reveal your weaknesses. These people are unlike jealous friends or relatives. These genuine souls care for you, care about your future, and constantly encourage you. These people are usually those you have known for years, and there is an obvious effort from both parties in cultivation of the relationship.

The benefits from the kind of true self-discovery that this section is discussing tie in with famed psychologist Dr. Abraham Maslow's Hierarchy of Needs concept. The lowest rung of Maslow's model is physical appetite, while the highest rung is self-actualization. Self-actualized individuals are fully aware of their beings and truest potential.

If your primary concerns are the banal concerns of the average student, you are not self-actualized. It would benefit you to look into Dr. Maslow's theory to help you discover yourself and achieve your long-term goals.

Offer yourself a true evaluation. Cherish your strengths and exploit them to the best of your ability. Meet your weaknesses head on. There is strength to be gained from knowing your weaknesses and then improving or mitigating them. A true self-assessment is critical to beginning your academic success. Before battle approaches, Sun Tzu considers knowing yourself and knowing your enemies of peak importance. An honest self-assessment is needed in order to know yourself as you approach your next battle (college).

## Writing Down the Goal-Oriented Plan

Take the time to write your plan. If a plan is not written down, as many political consultants will tell you, it is not a plan. Similarly, Military planners never undergo an operation without detailed, written plans.

The US Army uses operation orders. These are five-paragraph format plans. However, they are tentative. The commander's intent (for the end state of the operation) is always embedded within the second paragraph. Junior officers understand the commander's intent and amend the operation order to adapt to unforeseen, real-time situations. The commander's intent is constantly broken down to fit individual units but remains constant. The intent never changes, but the way in which subordinate units achieve this varies greatly based on mission, terrain, enemy, current situations, and limitations from other forms of guidance. Take a similar approach to your academic mission.

A well-written plan could be as sophisticated as a PowerPoint presentation or as simple as something scribbled on a legal pad. In the army, many people say, "a stubby pencil is better than a long memory." Although trite, the importance is retained. You will forget those things that are not recorded.

The main focus here is to set the fundament of your overall mission. Do not bog yourself down in this plan with too many specifics.

Develop your own commander's intent. Write down your base goals, such as having a 3.5 GPA first semester, joining organizations, graduating, getting your first job, and eventually being self-employed, and so forth. It will allow you to "put eyes on the objective" and see what you have yet to face. Before conducting an attack, a small unit leader always performs a reconnaissance where he looks at the objective while planning. You should do the same. Additionally, the written plans will allow you to assess where you are in the future. You can always reposition yourself, scratch out certain aspects, or keep on the same train.

A good technique is to write down your priorities and/or goals and put them somewhere you look often. This is very important. A military tactical operations center in the field at a domestic installation or in war is replete with graphics, goals, orders, and charts posted to the walls. These are posted in an operations center so that all the planners in the unit keep the mission specifics in mind as they meet the commander's intent during operations. Similarly, graphics will help you stay focused as you meet your own commander's intent of making the A grade.

Visual aids posted will also help when campaigning for office. Some politicians keep opponents' pictures in plain view at all times. They also have all sorts of maps and opponents' literature posted as well. Each one of these elements inspires a different emotion and a different thought.

Images put thoughts in our minds and constantly remind us of things. They keep us focused. Additionally, it is so easy to become absorbed in the daily work schedule. Visual images in your workspaces will greatly help you, whether you are a commander conducting a maneuver, a campaign manager, or a student seeking the A grade. Being able to reflect on your goals through pictures and illustrations will remind you of the goal you are working for now.

## Developing My Goals

Before we go any further, answer these basic questions. Please do not read any further until you have answered the following questions. How many course hours will I take the first two semesters? What GPA do I want the first Semester? How much time will I allow for social needs per week? How much time will I allow for studying per week?

I like to keep my graphics above my workspace at home. It is written down in a line graph that is annotated with goals five years out. The farthest I narrow it down is by month. Slicing it down any further would probably become time consuming, counter-productive, and maybe even discouraging.

However, be aware of guests and visitors. In guarding your future, it would not benefit you if people see these goals. Here you have your ambitions, hopes and dreams all spelled out for a person to use against you. Paranoid? Maybe. As they say in the PI field, "just because you are paranoid about someone following you, doesn't mean there is not someone following you." Jealously guard your dreams. The solution is simple; take them down when you have guests.

Always remember that even the most solid military and political plans need revising and amending from time to time. Finally, writing down a plan for your entire college career will give you extra confidence and peace of mind.

## Telling Other People

Tell other people about your goals once you have developed them and written down a general plan. Tell those trusted mentors confidently about your future plans for your life and your academic success. Limit the audience to these mentors. You will begin to develop confidence in your potential by reinforcing these goals through speech. This will also go a long way in dispelling personal doubts you may have. It will also be important not to isolate yourself from others through exuding a confidence that will be perceived as arrogance. This would undoubtedly isolate you from those valued mentors.

## Build on Past Success: A Shrine to Yourself

Always remember past success. Success in one area of your life has a tendency to spill over to other areas. You should always maintain a good way to remember past success.

I enlisted many mentors to help me accomplish my aims while an undergraduate. Lieutenant Colonel Chuck Hagan was one of the biggest influences. He was my ROTC battalion commander. It would be a separate book if I recorded all of the valuable advice he gave me. However, his advice on self-encouragement was key to me. Colonel Hagan told me to create a "me-wall." The idea is simple and is something I still use today.

Create a space for your achievements that is visible. Do this even if your crowded dorm room space is limited. I use a shelf and some wall space. I have all of my certificates framed and posted. All of my martial arts belts are on a rack. All of my course certifications are there. Pictures of people such as family adorn it as well.

Even the smallest achievements should be posted. Include things such as little league, peewee football, or junior basketball trophies and ribbons. I recently spoke about not gaining a false security from success in high school. However, if you had a stellar high school career, let it be reflected on your me-wall. Although those accomplishments will not directly affect your success in college, the self-confidence gained could serve invaluable. Anything you have won or accomplished deserves a spot on your me-wall.

The purpose of the wall is to prompt endurance. You will invariably become discouraged or disillusioned in college or throughout different seasons of life. Having a place to look at and reflect on your past success will encourage you to fight on. The wall will stand as a beacon for you to stay on your azimuth to success.

Essentially, use your past experience to propel you to success. Do not be coddled by past success but let yourself be magnified through a successful attitude. Keep the forward momentum. Self-assessment, writing goals down on paper, and telling mentors about your goals will all greatly enhance your chances of success in college. Always look to build. With each success under your belt, refit and reorganize for the next battle.

CHAPTER 2:

# THINKING TACTICALLY

**"Do not climb heights in order to fight. So much for mountain warfare."**

**-Sun Tzu**

Train yourself to think tactically. This means thinking deliberately. Before you ever even apply to college develop your stratagems for various situations. Rather than trying to be the "best student you can be," why not apply tactics that will put you over the edge? The purpose of college is to make "A"s. This book is not designed for you if your goal is learning and intellectual stimulation.

Stack the GPA deck. Fill in as many "A"s as you can. Do not take a class if you do not believe you can make an easy A in the class. You want "A"s at the end of the class or semester to enhance your subsequent pursuits. If you actually do learn something over the course of the class, then that is all the better.

Learning is not the primary goal. Getting the A grade is the primary goal. An example would be instructive. Student A learns a lot but struggles through and ends with Cs. Student B learns nothing but finishes with "A"s. Which individual would you be inclined to hire if all you had to go on was the grades? The starry-eyed pursuit of knowledge is not a consideration when you apply for a job. The GPA is an actual, recordable, and favored document on your performance and viability. Get the "A"s. Allow your competitors to climb those intellectual heights and wear themselves out over the course of the war.

Strategy is as much of a science as it is an art. In dealing with national defense, it is the military measures and political, economic, and psychological means to put a rival at the disadvantage and exploit him or her in peace or war. Apply this to your experience in college.

During summer break between my sophomore and junior year I worked as an assistant campaign manager for a local district race. This experience was invaluable because it taught me to think strategically. The full gamut of studying district maps, assessing voting strengths and weaknesses, and constant face-to-face campaigning gives a person unique insight.

The campaigning idealist tries to persuade and receive one hundred percent of the voters in a district. The campaigning realist assesses voting blocs and is careful on where to apply efforts. Similarly, you will attain the A. You will not accept the idealist's view to college, which focuses on intellectual development.

I directly took that experience with me and applied it to the rest of my college experience. Mountain warfare is an atrocious fight. It always has been. So is taking on impossible odds in the hard classes. So much for mountain warfare and intellectual challenges.

# CHAPTER 3:

# BEGINNING COLLEGE

**"If you know yourself but not the enemy, for every victory gained you will also suffer a defeat."**

**-Sun Tzu**

Beginning college is an overwhelming experience for even the most pre-pared student. It will be the first time he or she has to choose a particular field. It will also be an entirely new situation away from home and allies. The decisions you make will follow you. The most important thing to remember is to be decisive with yourself and consistent in your choices while going through this transition. Focus on getting as many "A"s and as many contacts as possible.

## Choosing a Major

When I began college, I did not know what I wanted to major in. I had my long-term specific goals in mind but did not have a plan for the immediate future. I learned very quickly to be decisive and choose the major that was best tailored to my aptitudes. I realized that in order to secure my long-term goals, I would need as many "A"s as possible.

I had learned my academic strengths and weaknesses by high school. I realized that a major that involved significant amounts of math would not be for me. I always excelled in government and social studies, so I chose political science. Stick with your instincts. If a particular major sounds impossible for you, then it probably is. Choose a major that you are certain will stimulate your interests and aptitudes.

If you are seeking a degree that requires technical skill sets, such as nursing, then you may not able to dodge all of the "hard" classes. It is important to note here that there is no such thing as "hard classes." Every person has different aptitudes and abilities, just as much as every class is attractive to a different type of person. For the purposes of this book, "hard classes" will be a catchall describing advanced math and sciences. Do not look at this as a setback; simply adjust your written plan accordingly.

The crucial thing to remember about a college degree (barring technical degrees) is that is just a credential. Never fool yourself into believing that you have to necessarily enter into a field related to your degree. For instance, music majors may be just as competent for business management as a business major in the real world.

Moreover, earning a political science degree in no way means that someone is capable of managing a campaign. In the real world, the chances of getting the job depend more on your personal contacts and the whole package of the individual than on a piece of paper showing a degree earned.

Think of your college major as a means to an end and not an end itself. The old adage, "if you believe in yourself, you can do anything!" should be discarded. You have already realized your potential, set concrete goals, and done a full introspective evaluation. This has allowed you to have a good handle on what you are made of. You are at the cusp of making hard right and left turns that will affect your adult life. Choose a major that you have the best chances of excelling in academically, and do not let yourself be fooled into any false expectations. It is time to believe in yourself, narrow down the specifics of your plan, and put it to action!

## Choosing Classes

Take care of the core prerequisites first when you begin college. Many students who neglect these core classes end up playing catch up toward their senior year. Ask the department for a print out of your core curriculum. Begin a checklist starting day one. Examine the entire document and understand it completely. Do not begin college by randomly taking classes. A commander would never enter into battle without an operation plan. Know exactly what classes you need to take. Nothing you do from this point should be random. Everything will be deliberate.

Your core classes include the basic sciences, English, math, and so forth. These will be 101 "confidence building" classes that allow you to get the feel for the college arena. Be sure to take these early and enroll in them early, as the rest of the freshman class will be enrolling there as well.

## Advisors

Never put faith in advisors. Intentions aside, advisors often confuse the student more than they help. Some advisors are sharp and offer great advice; most, however, do not. A college is often a bloated bureaucracy, and advisors are custodians of that arrangement. This is not meant to be a harangue against advisors. These are some realities that must be considered.

Bureaucracies' goals are administrative convenience rather than efficiency. Consider the advisor himself: you are among his many concerns. He gets paid the same no matter what the quality and quantity of his work. It suits his interests to "put people in seats" rather than taking the time to consider each instance and individual thoughtfully.

Never listen to any advice from advisors who encourage you to challenge yourself by taking impossible classes. Your goal should be to enroll in the classes that you have the best chances of making "A"s. The advisors have nothing to lose here, but you do! For all you know, this person is attempting to fill an unpopular class for an unpopular teacher he or she plays golf with on the weekends.

At the end of the day, your transcripts will show grades bottom line. They will not reflect lofty but noble attempts at self-discovery. You alone are responsible for advancing your own interests and goals. Always opt for the easy A over the adventure in self-discovery.

Additionally, many advisors are instructed by departments to fill classes for the sake of the university or college. They may tell you that you need a class when you really do not. This could cause you to miss out on an opportunity for taking a class tailored to your goals and aptitudes. Put your interests above the university's needs. Only by acting as your own advisor can you be certain that your best interests are put to the forefront.

It is much more effective to obtain a registrar guide and choose the classes for yourself. Always remember to annotate the classes you signed up for and have taken on the core curriculum sheet. This core curriculum sheet can act as advisor during your college career. Consider it part of your written plan. Make copies and file it away accordingly.

I kept the core curriculum checklist with me from the first day at university to graduation. Throughout college, I would cross out what I had taken. It was actually very therapeutic to do this. It is like a rat slowly nibbling away at a hunk of cheese. As time goes the list gets smaller and smaller. Once you have completed a class, you take out your pen and literally check the box. You feel accomplished and are constantly reminded of progress.

Always remember that you are training to be a goal-driven and a self-reliant person. It is always fine to ask for help. However, never totally entrust your class schedule to an advisor.

## Balancing Social and Academic Concerns

It is easy to have an abundant social life and a successful academic life at the same time. I am not professing to be a therapist or a counselor on emotional health. That is a separate book. However, this section is largely based on observations of successful students and their less fortunate counterparts.

Timing is the key here. If your primary goal in college is to "have a good time," or advance your social success, then this book is not for you. Your primary concern should be success, and then allow your social needs to follow as a secondary concern.

New college students are as bombarded with invitations from social organizations as they are attracted by the bright lights of the newest club in town. It is good for you to take part in as many social activities as your schoolwork will allow.

## Develop a Strict Schedule

Never mix work time and play time. Treat your academic concerns as you would if it were work for pay. Once you have your classes assigned, create a tight schedule.

In college, I began my mornings at 5:30 a.m. I would conduct physical training (PT) with my ROTC detachment. The prospect of this seemed rather daunting at first, but I learned to appreciate it as another means to strengthen my mind and body and obtain my long-term goals.

I will never forget many of the words my mentor LTC Hagan told us as cadets. He was famous for his motivational speeches. He once told us after a long and grueling run, "You all made a conscious and deliberate decision this morning! You rolled out of your beds before daylight, while the rest of the campus is racked out, and decided to come to formation!" Conscious decision really resonated with me.

He continued, "Life will be a series of deliberate decisions. You can rest assured that you are learning a lot about self-discipline right now!" Conscious and deliberate. I still think about those words often. I can see now that he was teaching us not only to make the right decisions but , was reminding us to own our decisions.

I made the conscious decision to have a disciplined life. After PT, I would eat and shower. By eight o' clock, I had exercised, showered, eaten, and read the campus paper, all while other students were still sleeping. By the time I came to class later in the day, I was fully awake and prepared to conquer the work before me.

This morning schedule may not be for everyone. However, it is important to develop a similar one that suits your particular needs. The importance here is routine. Find one and stick to one that works for you.

Ultimately, through a strict schedule, I swam against the current of average students. Most of my colleagues' schedules involved a drowsy wake up at 11:00 a.m., a groggy appearance to class after lunch, an afternoon nap, and a night of debauchery to end the day.

Do the opposite of the crowd. When your mother or some other mentor told you to not follow the crowd, she was onto something. I took this lesson and applied it to my time in college. I used the terminology of current for a reason. Currents shift and flow with the sea. The herd shifts and flows with a similarly strong pattern that threatens to pull us in and drown us. Always swim against the current. Whatever the majority of students is doing is probably not the thing you should be doing. After all, it is energizing to realize how much work you are accomplishing while your competition is sleeping.

## Put in Full Work Days

Never waste time during the day. Exploit the precious time you will have in between classes. Your only breaks should be breakfast and lunch, whatever schedule you keep. Napping can wait. Many students foolishly squander their precious time conversing in coffee shops or remaining back at the dorm asleep.

Fill in the gaps with schoolwork because there is always something else to be done. For instance, look at your syllabi and take care of menial Internet homework that is due the next week. You could also begin reading and outlining/highlighting chapters in your textbooks.

When you put in a full day's work, you will be able to rest easier at night and better prepare yourself for the next day's mission. Academic work requires constant study. If you keep to a schedule based on full workdays (at least four hours of independent outside-of-class work per day), you will dominate in the academic arena.

## Getting Exposure

Be seen studying constantly. There is a subtle importance to this. First, having an audience can be energizing. Second, your competition will be discouraged. Lastly, your professors will see you. Exposure is very important.

We should look at Benjamin Franklin's early life for an instructive example. As a young man, Benjamin Franklin would do certain things in public in order to be perceived as a hard worker. He started up a small stationers' operation in Philadelphia. He would dress in modest attire. He would very carefully put on the appearance to other, more established merchants that he was prudent and diligent. To secure this image, he would never be seen fishing, relaxing, or distracting himself from his business. He would even go so far as to push a wheelbarrow past window fronts in town. A review of his autobiography would be instructive. These displays secured his business contacts and promoted his reputation. To you, other people's perceptions of you should be at least as important as they were to this Forefather.

Locate and target key places (high-traffic areas) on campus. Follow Mr. Franklin's example. This is best reserved for those times that you are "filling in the gaps" between classes. Save your serious study (i.e., tests) for more private locations. Franklin was not on the streets of Philadelphia announcing business strategy. He was on the streets displaying his industry. Similarly, you do not need to allow your competition to view your actual studying tactics.

Good high-traffic areas include sitting on the steps of the library, outside pavilion areas, etc. Other students witness your conduct as well as your professors. Soon you will establish a solid reputation for being a hard worker. Externally, this benefits you because you discourage your competition. Also, you create the image in your professor's mind that you are a talented and diligent student.

Internally, you will be reinforcing your success. When people begin to see you as a hard worker, you will be reassured yourself. You will hear them tell you this. As Thoreau wrote, "No man is an island unto himself..." Allow this to build on your own self-confidence.

## Claim Time to Relax and Reenergize

No operation or unit can continue to fight constantly. The *US Army Field Manual 100-5* directs, "...the necessity for conservation of the fighting power of the troops requires provision for the periodic relief of units in line." As an army cadet and a student on a specific mission, I always found it important to claim time for myself to relax. Just as in war, we cannot keep fighting forever. Now, as an officer in the army, I find it even more important to claim time for myself. We must refit and reorganize at some point.

It is highly important to enjoy life and to enjoy friendships. Do not be afraid to put your schoolwork down on the weekends and make time for yourself. This lesson is most important for the most-driven students, although it may be hard for these people to make time to reenergize.

Use your weekends as a tool to enhance your academic success. It is a lot easier to work hard during the week if you realize that you can play harder on the weekends. After you put your honest week of work in, punch out on Friday afternoons and do not return until Monday morning!

I can count on one hand how many times I had to study on the weekends in my entire undergraduate study. This is a testament to forward planning and keeping a strict schedule during the week. If you put in enough work during the week, then you do not have to settle the balance on the weekends.

The herd has usually relaxed all week and uses weekends to cram and play catch up. You will not fall into this pattern. You are swimming against the current.

Go a step further and actually do not even think about schoolwork on the weekend. If you consider a great weekend to be a trip to the beach or lying on a recliner, then do it.

Always be careful. There is nothing that can halt your chances of success like a DUI or a misdemeanor charge. These incidents happen in the blink of an eye, and no one ever plans on them happening. Use your best judgment, travel in buddy teams, and if a situation makes you uncomfortable, then leave.

Once again, it does not hurt to be seen having a good time when you're considered a top-notch student. It is not very common to find a straight-A student who has an ample social life. People may wonder how you have both but do not understand the work you have put in all week.

The simple key to this is to save it ALL for the weekend. This means declining any invitation to any late night activity or escapade on school nights. Besides, this will only add to the catharsis after a good work-week. Always attempt to be well rounded. Chiefly, never mix work time with playtime, but play as hard as you work.

CHAPTER 4:

# LONG-RANGE PLANNING

**"We are not fit to lead an army on the march unless we are familiar with the face of the country."**

**-Sun Tzu**

Long range planning is essential for all forms of success. In war, commanders extensively plan for the attack. This process ensures synchronization of his combat power on the objective through the military decision-making process and troop-leading procedures. Combat power encompasses all resources available to the commander. This includes soldiers, weapon systems, indirect fire assets, air assets, radar, and intelligence. Only a foolish commander would randomly assign an asset to respond to an enemy attack or initiate aggressive movement against a dug-in enemy. The commander has already established a plan to maximize, arrange, and combine all of these assets to affect the greatest lethality on the enemy and maximize his own resources.

Planning for success in college requires a good understanding of the syllabi. Study your syllabi in depth the first few days of class. Study them at home or in a private place.

Read everything on them from cover to cover. Read one syllabus at a time. In so doing, you will have a picture of and a grasp on the class itself. The professor's intent is explicitly outlined, and it is an effective tool to assess the professor's personality and overall mood of the class. Students who neglect the syllabi disadvantage themselves gravely. The syllabus is a road map to your viability in the class.

## Battle Map

Make a battle map. In the world of armed conflict, battle maps include terrain, models, and graphics. The maps we use in the military are topographical and superimposed with a myriad of graphics. Some of these graphics included range indicator rings for different weapon systems, individual units' areas of responsibility, intelligence concerns, and civilian infrastructure.

For the academic world, your map should include key information. Every known assignment, from quizzes to final exams, should be represented. A map will save you from forgetting an assignment and give you peace of mind. Additionally, the map will protect you against feeling overwhelmed early on in the semester.

The map can be as simple as a large calendar. Buy a calendar that is at least three feet by three feet and post it to a wall where you do the most work. Take one syllabus at a time and begin to write down all assignments in the calendar blocks. Use a different-colored marker for each class. This will stop you from confusing classes.

Include school breaks, such as spring break and Christmas. This will allow you to look forward to some very much-needed repose. You should have every assignment, test, homework paper, essay, and break from August to December for a fall semester marked on the calendar.

Add to or delete from your map as you see fit during the course of the semester. However, do not post non-academic concerns there. Use another calendar for that. This is your battle map, and it is best not cluttered with doctors' appointments and other menial engagements. Simplicity is a principle of war and should not be ignored here. Your focus will be crystallized in relation to how simple your battle map is.

Place an X as you complete assignments. This will add to your sense of accomplishment when you can see how much work you have done as the semester develops. Whether you are a visual learner or not, the battle map can be an outstanding way to prepare for the long term while benefiting from past work accomplished that you can actually see.

## Degree Layout

It is time to refine your overall plan of getting an A in each class even more. Ask your department secretaries if degree-planning sheets are available. Make your own if your university does not offer them. Retrieve a university course catalogue regardless.

One great approach is as follows: With a pen or software (such as Excel), put two boxes on a page. Each box represents one semester while each page represents an academic year. Ensure the boxes have at least five lines, one for each prospective class. Copy your first enrollment into the first box, as it is your first semester. Look at classes offered that you will need for the following semester. You should look at your particular degree's core curriculum sheet and begin filling in the prerequisites and other core classes you need for the next semester. You now have your first year of college planned out in earnest.

Next, you should apply this same approach to your following semesters, all the way to graduation. Remember to take the basic 101 requirements first. To be certain, your current catalogue will only show classes that are offered for a certain period (usually one full academic year). Nonetheless, do the best work possible in filling in the rest of your classes. As previously mentioned, much like a syllabus, long-range planning is tentative. You can always go back later and amend your degree layout.

The importance of this task is similar to the battle map. It allows you to gear up for upcoming semesters and helps you achieve valuable peace of mind.

One of the best benefits of constructing a degree plan from day one to graduation is that you will not become overwhelmed at the end. If done correctly, your degree plan will ensure that you will never take more than an average of fifteen hours (five classes) per semester. More than likely, you will actually end up only needing nine or twelve hours in your final semesters.

Countless students neglect long-range planning and end up taking absurd numbers of classes in order to graduate. This approach is a waste of money and time, and it hurts your chances of finishing college with solid "A"s. A degree plan is a good start in avoiding this obstacle altogether.

The more classes you take, the harder it will be to make all "A"s. If you end up playing the catch-up game at the end, you will probably have to take nineteen hours or more. This is because rather than massing your fires on one target (class) for the optimum effect, you have to undergo an economy of force. Economy of force is another principle of war, where a commander uses the minimum amount of resources on secondary concerns in order to focus resources on a primary target. Your goal is to mass fires on each class. This is not difficult when taking a comfortable amount of hours per semester. The degree plan is essential to long-range planning.

**CHAPTER 5:**

# PERCEPTION

**"Pretend to be weak, that he may grow arrogant."**

**-Sun Tzu**

The research paper is one of the most valuable targets to exploit when making all "A"s. You must bolster the effect of your paper once you have put in the academic legwork. This will be accomplished by being precise and accurate in your research citations.

This section will provide you with the tools to write an excellent paper. It will not be an in-depth discussion of effective writing. There are millions of books on that subject. This chapter will focus on the missing element of those books: "working on the professor." This term means demonstrating your virtues to the professor in ways similar to young Benjamin Franklin's approaches to merchants. Your virtues will be hard-work ethic; willingness to learn; and good, old-fashioned manners.

The professor will be much more inclined to giving you the A grade when she sees these virtues you demonstrate through the paper-writing process. However, this must be complemented with long-term planning and old-fashioned, solid academic work.

Researching for papers is a means of targeting. Targets are divided by priority in the field of US Army targeting. Targets range from targets of opportunity to high payoff targets. For instance, a high payoff target would be a high-ranking Taliban financier who funds many different projects. Neutralizing him is a high payoff for the overall US mission. The efforts to neutralize him are multiplied through the subsequent termination of his projects which otherwise would have sustained the enemy war effort.

## Choose a Topic Early

Narrow down a topic as early as possible. This should be easy since you have already dissected your syllabus and implemented a battle map. You will notice papers due months in advance, before they are ever mentioned verbally in the class. Go to the professor and discuss a topic. Preferably, about two months before the paper is due, narrow down your choices to three or fewer. Your display of scholarly virtue will begin in earnest when you meet with the professor to discuss a research topic months in advance.

Schedule an appointment with the professor, as face-to-face contact is the best form of communication. E-mails are flippant. They do not demonstrate virtue. You want to indicate that you are taking her class very seriously at all times. Subsequently, this implies that you take the individual seriously as well.

Face-to-face meetings have another great effect. These engagements allow the professor to learn your name early, and more chiefly, put a face to a name in the grade book. The professor sees an ocean's worth of faces on a daily basis. These young faces become indistinct and muddled in the hallways and from the podium view. Take this easy opportunity to stand out from your competition.

Ask the professor politely, "Ma'am, I've been thinking about this paper in your class and have narrowed it down to two topics." Emphasize "your" class to enhance her ego. At best, your topic will meet her requirements and you will seem competent. At worst, you realize that your topic needs improvement, and you show the professor that you're willing to work. You win either way.

There are three important benefits to choosing a topic early. First, you get an initial feel for what the professor is looking for in the paper. Your initial topic may be too broad at first, and it is essential to narrow it down for research purposes. Second, you will impress the professor by standing out among your peers.

Remember secrecy. Don't frequent your professor's office so much that other students will notice. Sun Tzu spoke of a wise military commander, "He carries out his own secret designs, keeping his antagonists in awe." They would rightfully assume you are a suck-up if discovered. Strategic times such as Friday afternoons works best. One, all students are in mass exodus from campus after lunch. Two, the professor is shocked that you are so interested in your studies that your will come in on a Friday afternoon. This behavior is irregular and wins the praise of your professors. You are swimming against the current of the herd. Additionally, and most significantly, none of your competition has any idea what you are doing.

Most of your peers will be storming the professor's office two weeks before the assignment is due. It is important to stand out from the masses of students for your teacher, while blending in as far as the other students are concerned. It is almost a guarantee that the professor is used to seeing students year after year waiting until the last minute. You have planted the seed in the professor's mind, a month before she marks your grade on the paper, that you are highly diligent.

Third, and most importantly, you have begun to establish a rapport with the professor. She can much more easily associate a face with a name.

By virtue of human nature, it is always much easier to benefit those you like and slight those who you do not. Your rapport will be buttressed by tactics described in further lessons. Most students will never understand how many aspects of getting "A"s are involved in things as simple as "choosing a topic early." For the sake of making the A, keep it that way!

## Gathering Research

Begin to gather sources immediately once you have chosen a topic. Gathering research is a necessary evil and should not be taken lightly. Researching seems conventional compared to the tactics you will learn to make "A"s in this book. However, there are no shortcuts to the rigors that good research requires. There are no clever tricks or tactics that will substitute for hard work and studying.

In a political campaign, a candidate must hit the pavement and endure the heat and ravenous guard dogs to knock on voters' doors in order to win. General Omar Bradley's words are instructive here: "Amateurs talk tactics, professionals study logistics." Gathering quality research is paramount. This cannot be said often enough. For a research paper, think of this legwork as logistics. The library is the ammo supply point, and your research paper is the forward line of troops. In order to wage a successful campaign, a commander must have all of his supplies met with all of his soldiers in an opportune manner. Similarly, you must gather your supplies (books, etc.) in a timely manner in order to ensure the A grade. It will probably be the most time-consuming portion of your writing process.

Begin checking out as many books as possible and printing out as many online journals as possible. For instance, for a ten-page paper, check out eight books and print out ten journal articles. First, these numbers are important because it will take that many to decide which particular sources you will actually use. Attack it early. You will feel much better and be fully prepared once you get ready to put pen to paper.

## Use Frivolous Internet Sources Only for Getting Started

Use Wikipedia or other frivolous Internet sites to get a grasp of the subject matter if you do not know much about your topic. It is good to use the Internet initially because it is so much easier to read than books or journal articles. This frees your time to handle many projects at once in the early stages of the semester. The key to this initial inquiry is only to help you become familiar with, not well versed, on the subject at hand. Mediocre research will earn mediocre grades. Essentially, only look at non-scholarly Internet sites as a preliminary measure but never use them as a citation in any paper.

## Using Books and Online Scholarly Journals

Books and scholarly journals are your primary sources of information. Your goal is to have as many scholarly sources buttressing the bibliography as possible. Anybody can cite random and unsubstantiated websites in a bibliography. You are looking to demonstrate solid research to your professor. Remember that the research is just as important as the content.

Go to your library and check out at least eight books for a ten-page paper. This is not the rule, only a good benchmark. You have to gather a lot of books because you will probably find only two or three out of the seven are worthwhile. Using books for research means using the index. If a book does not have an index, discard it. For instance, imagine your topic is "Beauregard's failure to implement the turning movement in the Battle of Shiloh." Look in the index for key words. Here, the obvious key words are "Shiloh," "Turning Movement," and "Beauregard." The prospect of using books can be daunting at first, but will be greatly rewarding in helping you get an A paper. Once you begin to use the index, you will find how easy and helpful they can be.

Online scholarly journals are sometimes better than books for a research project. This is so because they are brief and more specific. You may even find several journal articles that match your subject and thesis almost exactly. For instance, we are writing our General Beauregard paper. There are a plethora of other scholars who have written in-depth analyses on Gen. Beauregard's failure to execute the turning movement at Shiloh. There are also other similar articles that can give you added perspective. On the other hand, after finding general terms in the index of a book, you must read into to it to discover the desired specifics. This can be very time-consuming and cumbersome. Online scholarly journals are a great tool because they are easily accessed on the Internet and carry the same scholarly weight as books for research.

Online journals can be accessed through the academic search engines available in your university library. Your university pays monthly prescriptions for these. Print out as many of these as you deem relevant.

Lay your printouts in front of you at your workspace. I always preferred to use the floor in front of me. Skim over them. Read the introductions and at least the first line of each paragraph. Highlight and underline anything you think might be relevant to your subject. Write the author's name in large print across the top of the cover page using a brightly colored marker. This will help you keep them separate while writing and make the final reference citing much easier.

## Creating a Bibliography

Most students will probably rely most heavily on Internet sites. Their bibliographies will include crude and lazy looking research and be riddled with ".com" sources. This is great for you because when the professor finally gets to your paper, she will see painstaking research.

Exercise discretion and care when citing a book or article written by the professor herself. I advise against this. However, if you must, be careful. There two parameters to consider. First, your professor will know the subject she wrote about inside and out. She may actually be offended if you take her words out of the context she intended.

Second, if a student does this to impress the instructor, he or she has failed. This would be rather lazy and very transparent. Your professor is likely to be highly seasoned and calloused from the traditional "suck-up students."

The following is the best method, if you feel you need to cite her work. A good way to do this is to annotate her class lecture notes. Only once per paper is sufficient. In college, I wrote notes every day and had the date assigned to each set of notes. Your professor deserves to be cited, as she is an expert in her field.

Citing actual class lecture notes in your bibliography will do two things: First, it will show how organized you are and how much you care about what they have to say. Not to mention, your competition probably would never dream of doing so, even if they actually had written class notes.

Second, and most importantly, it will allow the professor to glow by seeing her name cited. This will promote feelings of accomplishment within her. It will make her feel heard and important. Citing a class lecture from them will definitely testify that you appreciate them.

The research itself is a large part of the battle. It is the framework from which you will launch your final plan. Think of it as a strategic tool to help you stand out from the mass of students and get your well-deserved A paper.

## Beginning a Rough Draft

The first thing you need to do is to just write something—anything. The hardest part of writing is getting started. Ideas will be sure to follow once you take the leap and put pen to paper. Creative thought is stimulated through the physical act of writing or typing.

While you are writing, your competition is probably not. Remember this and let it encourage you. You will benefit in the end, since you had the foresight to act strategically. Think about all of the students who have not even looked at the assignment on the syllabus, much less have begun any research. Let this be a source of inspiration. You do not have to worry because you are putting yourself to the forefront of the professor's respect. Additionally, you can always scrap it and start over. The importance here is that you will begin to come up with ideas as you write.

## While Writing

Justify your thesis statement and keep your thoughts in a clear order while writing a rough draft. Keep a loose copy of your outline near your battle map as you write. Refer to it often.

## Thesis Statement

The thesis statement is the sum of your paper. This concept is well known but is lost on many college writers. Your thesis is only one sentence—the very first sentence. Do not include anything in there that you will not prove or argue in the actual paper. For instance, if I were assigned a paper on why the US lost in the Vietnam Conflict, I would refine my thesis and develop provable claims. A bad thesis would be: "The United States lost in Vietnam for many reasons. One reason was the government's alienation of the military, and another is the people's loss of faith in the war back home." On the other hand, a good thesis would be: "The United States lost in Vietnam because of its failure to adhere to the Clausewitzean trinity of the government, the military, and the people." The instructor has a clear anticipation of what the rest of the story is about. She will anticipate at least three subsequent body headings on the government, military, and people. Just as a commander is compelled by the principle of war—simplicity—to give understandable and uncomplicated orders, you should take the same approach to your thesis.

## Use an Outline

Create an outline before writing. This is the only effective way to organize your thoughts. In the army, all operations orders are in the standard five-paragraph form. An officer fills in the preset blocks. These blocks are: situation, mission, execution, sustainment, and command

and signal. This arrangement greatly mitigates confusion and ensures logical and uncomplicated orders.

Similarly, create your own operation order when writing your paper. The five-paragraph format that the US Army uses in every mission from the highest to lowest level of planners contains situation, mission, execution, service and support, and command and signal. Consider the following hypothetical example for your mission:

**Situation**: Research paper is due on October 31, 2015. The current date is September 28, 2015. I have gathered sources and am now creating an outline and rough draft. There are two other history papers due this semester. My professor is the sole audience of the paper.

**Mission**: My mission is to receive an A on this paper.

**Execution**: I will write an A paper by creating my own deadlines. I will complete my rough draft by October 13. I will proofread the rough draft and submit it to the professor for review October 14. I will implement the professor's suggestions and proofread one final time and create final copies no later than October 26. I will file the final draft in my class folder and e-mail a reserve copy to myself no later than October 28.

**Sustainment**: Online databases available through Starlight search engine. Librarian staff is on reserve. Campus writing labs located west of library in Eagle Hall.

**Command and Signal:** Printer connection and availability is best in Stout Hall. Internet connection is best in library. This logical order will help you understand the approach to writing a college paper. This is the minimum of considerations that you should keep in mind when planning to write an A paper.

Making an outline is simple. Tear out a blank sheet of paper and have your sources at hand. Use the roman numeral approach beginning with your thesis. Each new roman numeral should be one sentence and your next thought. Write down supporting ideas as needed under each topic. Review and skim your sources to find headers for the supporting paragraphs. Annotate your outline next to the underlying idea, using the author's name and page number.

An outline is simple but will take some time. It forces you to clear all of the sources you have gathered. It gives you one-line sentences to keep all of your subsequent ideas fluid. The outline is critical to writing the A paper.

## Topic Sentences

Stick to your outline throughout the paper-writing process. Stay disciplined and underscore your topic sentences with relevant substance. Ensure all of your paragraphs are streamlined and follow a topic sentence. Observe the following excerpt from a scholarly paper:

"The crucial shortfall in the Clausewitzean trinity was the American people. Colonel Summers said that the government's failure to mobilize domestic support was one of the most important strategic failures in the Vietnam conflict (Summers 19). The Tet Offensive, the American media, and the organized anti-war movement all played a large role in the erosion of the national will to support the war."

The topic sentence here is "The crucial shortfall in the Clausewitzean trinity was the American people." This is explicit and states an idea to be proven. This topic sentence will be proven by the following three paragraphs. The Tet Offensive, the American media, and the organized antiwar movement will all be subsequent topic paragraphs. Each one of these subsequent paragraphs will prove the original topic sentence.

Continue the rest of your writing in this logical fashion. Your goal is to never allow the professor to be confused while reading your paper. If you do not follow this logical order, then you will not receive an A on your paper.

## Consider Your Language Style

Always use active voice. This takes place when the subject is doing the action. Take the following sentences for instance: "Ted ran through the hills. The vines slapped him as he ran through the foliage." This language is direct and readable. A poor way to express this idea would be, "When Ted was running through the hills, he was slapped by the vines as he ran in the entangled foliage."

The latter is passive language. "He was slapped by," and "When," are unnecessary. Never use passive language because it detracts from your language, thus diluting your message. It is best to make a long sentence into two where possible.

## Overcoming Writer's Block

Writer's block is sure to become a thorn in your side at some point in the process. However, you can overcome writer's block with a variety of methods. The first good way to overcome writer's block is to reach a stopping point and come back to it later. Since you have started early, you have the time to write in a piecemeal fashion. Choose a time that is right for you and feel free to stop when you lose focus. Starting early allows you to write the best content possible with a clear and relaxed mind.

A second good way to beat writer's block is to read something else that is outside of the subject matter at hand. Free your mind and creativity by picking up a novel or any literature that is unrelated to your paper. This is an effective means of generating new thoughts and a new vigor. For instance, it would be fine to break from a sixteenth-century American colonial paper and pick up *Lord of the Rings*. Since you have planned ahead, you have the freedom to relax, consolidate your thoughts, and reorganize. However, do not get too lost in a new book and neglect your paper!

## Hammer out the Rough Drafts

A thorough review follows a first draft. There are no shortcuts to finishing a rough draft. In battle, commanders take calculated risks to mitigate loss of supplies and human resources. However, losses will occur. Soldiers will be sent to the front, into the trenches, and on long patrols through enemy territory. Many will perish, but hopefully the mission will be complete and ground will be occupied. Treat your rough draft this way. You will spend much time hacking away through the dark jungles of academia, fighting foes as writers block and distraction but ultimately emerging victorious and holding your ground.

Once you spend the hours needed to crank out a rough draft, consider it territory won. You have finally established a beachhead into the enemy's country and you are now prepared to mount a large-scale assault to finish him off. Your eyes and brain will be strained at the end, but you will have conquered key terrain in completing the daunting rough draft.

## Review

Reviewing your rough draft is as important as getting it done promptly. You, a friend, and the professor should all take part in this. First, print out several copies of your first draft. Not only will you have hard copies in case your computer crashes, but it will also give you a better view of it. A hard copy allows you to circle, mark out, and make notes all over the paper. All rough drafts will need many revisions. One of the best revisions is taking out any filler. Brevity retains meaning. It is time to put any pride aside and begin slicing out whole sentences and paragraphs.

Key things to watch for are superfluous words and random sentences. Keep a balance in your diction. On the one hand, you want to sound scholarly and formal, and on the other you do not want to sound pretentious. Usually, the former should yield to the latter. It is always better to use simple words rather than words that impress. Remember that getting the message across to your audience is the most important thing.

Your sole audience is the professor. She probably knows every word in the dictionary and will likely be taken aback by flowery language.

Your one goal should be to get an A. If you want to take liberties in flowery language, save it for your personal time! Never lose sight of the goal. Feel free to use a formal academic word when it feels appropriate, but when revising it is best to replace those with more common words. Why say "the Jefferson's steeds were purloined by the provincial marauders in Lee's woods" when you could say, "The local robbers stole the Jefferson's horses?" The contrast here is obvious.

Continue to slice! Any sentence or phrase unrelated to a topic sentence should be removed. Think of good writing as a flowing stream. There are bends and turns, but there is a constant forward momentum toward the mouth. Similarly, your writing should be fluidly moving toward completing your thesis with a conclusion. Sentences that seem awkward or irrelevant are dikes and dams interrupting the flow of your paper. Dynamite those obstacles by slashing out any irrelevant filler sentences.

CHAPTER 6:

# KEY TARGETS

**"Men who are anxious to win the favor of a Prince nearly always follow the custom of presenting themselves to him with the possessions they value most..."**

**-Niccolo Machiavelli**

Your grades are at the sole discretion of your professor or instructor. For the most part, your professors will be keenly aware of how to deal with students. With thousands of students over the course of a career, professors are highly aware of the difference between a good student and a poor student.

However, professors are susceptible to the innate vulnerabilities in human nature that the ancients wrote about. It does not take much effort to put yourself to the forefront of your professor's graces and rise above the masses of average students. In this section we will discuss fellow students, professors, and support staff as key targets.

## Competition

Be aware of your competition. Your competition is the other class-mates. This may sound somewhat sinister, but it is a frame of mind that is essential. This does not mean that you should have bad relations with other classmates. Neither does it mean that you should do anyone else any harm at all. It means that while being friendly and blending in, you should rise above the fray. You can be respectful and kind to other students without allowing them to gain an advantage over you. This can be achieved through out working them fair and square.

## Your Professor as a Key Target: How to Win the Professor

Your professor is the sole keeper of the grade book. She is totalitarian in her control of the flow of "A"s that ends up on papers and finals. Your professor is the most critical target.

# First Impressions

Making a good first impression with your instructor is paramount. Go out of your way—on the first day or the first available day—to introduce yourself. This early meeting will begin to distinguish you from the rest of the faceless masses that congregate for class on a daily basis. This effort will not only put a face to a name for your professor but will also show her that you believe she is important enough to meet personally.

In the military and as a young officer (lieutenant or second lieutenant), first-time meetings with a new commander will shape your relationship with him. This is also the case with subordinates.

A new lieutenant is the leader of a platoon. He relies heavily on his non-commissioned officers (NCOs) to execute his plans and drive the soldiers. NCOs are a much more hardened cut of soldier than the Officer Corpse. NCOs will tell you up front how they feel about something or if someone or something (including you) is "ate up" or "jacked up."

I knew the first impression on my commander and my subordinates would be crucial to my efficacy in the unit. I used firm body language, strong handshakes, determined but caring eyes, and a willingness to listen as weapons against being written off as a flake. Let the other person do most of the talking. Saying too much will leave a bad taste in the other person's mouth for you.

Demonstrating to others that you are willing to listen does three things: First, it shows that you believe what they have to say is important. Second, it shows that you believe they are important. Finally, it shows that you are flexible and able to understand that person. Good listeners are very rare. You will not only shock the other person, but you will automatically fall into his or her good graces merely by listening to him or her and showing great interest in his or her words (in him or her).

First impressions are everything. Establish a good impression at all costs and as early as possible. If you have implemented the guidance from previous chapters, then you should be fine.

## Getting a Feel for Your Professor

Get a feel for the type of person your professor is and what she wants. Give that image to her once you have assessed it. I once asked an old politician what the secret of appealing to voters was. He said, "If he's a drinking man, then give him a little whiskey." This may sound repulsively superficial to some. In fact, I was repulsed by it at the time until I realized what it meant. There is a lot of wisdom there. The importance for you is to find out what the professor wants in a student and what kind of writing, products, and answers she wants. Give her all of it.

However, how can you give your professors what they want if you haven't conducted the information gathering on what they want? The way to acquire this information is through reconnaissance and surveillance. Reconnaissance is a specific mission conducted in order to get confirmation on specific persons, activities, or places.

Surveillance is mostly observation of movement of surface areas. The *US Army Field Manual 3-21.21* instructs a commander that reconnaissance and surveillance are a continuous process that should be conducted twenty-four hours a day. Granted, you will not be able to conduct these twenty-four hours a day. However, you should conduct surveillance and reconnaissance as much as your situation allows. This continuous process occurs inside and outside of class.

# In-Class Conduct Surveillance

Listen and pay attention to the way your professor responds to other students. Some professors invite questions and open discussion. Others are not interested in this at all. The former usually respects pertinent and creative questions. Asking superficial and obnoxious questions is received poorly by students and teachers alike. Everyone looks with discomfort and disgust to that person in the class who hijacks the session with constant, frivolous questions. There has been one of these individuals in your class ever since elementary school. Do not be this person.

A good rule is to ask one creative and thought-provoking question per class. Ask the question that will make you appear to be critical. Remember, the goal here is not seeking knowledge but creating a very specific image of you. Be shrewd in the delivery and timing of these questions. Never seem abrupt. Use pauses for effect. Always stay in line with the main point at issue or topic of discussion.

The type of professor who usually invites questions and discussion is often younger. Older professors tend to like lecture format. They have been teaching the same material for a great many years by this point. The seniors usually want to give you fifty minutes of lecture with minimal input from you. If you sense that they do not want input, then do not try to give it to them. Never force it.

Younger professors typically encourage more discussion and interaction, on the other hand. The young instructor is learning her own teaching style and still has ideals. Take advantage of this arrangement.

Conclusively, if your professor wants questions, be the one to offer up the creative question that will dazzle them and others. If your professor wants to lecture for fifty minutes, be the quiet mouse. Always remember, "If he's a drinking man, give him a little whiskey..."

## Reconnoitering Outside of Class (in the Field)

Pay attention to everything about your professors. A SALT report is standard military doctrine to record information. The acronym goes as follows: size; actions being taken; location; time of occurrence.

Use a similar format as you mentally create a file on each of your professors. SALT reports are a format to organize raw data. Raw data is information. Information is given by units in the field to intelligence cells that act as clearing houses to produce intelligence. Intelligence is raw data pieced together to paint a clear picture of enemy dispositions, terrain considerations, and other fundamental elements needed for operations planning.

You will need to collect raw data in the field and piece it together with other forms of information in order to create an intelligent profile of your professors. One good way to do this is to pay very close attention to conspicuous signs. This includes things like affiliation stickers, type of car, or pins or badges worn. You will be able to record a lot of information in that brief time.

When you are in one of your professor's office, examine the room carefully. A few general questions to keep in mind are as follows; Are things neat? Are things cluttered? If things are neat, then does that mean that she is anal retentive about the details? If the desks are cluttered, does that mean she is unconcerned with details and more prone to creativity? This is a basic but effective form of intelligence gathering.

All information can be used. All of this raw information can undergo the clearing process in your mind and combined with other small pieces of information you have received from other means, including in-class surveillance. Eventually, you will have a very accurate profile of your professor.

# Arguing with the Professor?

Arguing with the professor over subject matter or a topic of discussion should be done with great finesse. As with questions in class, give your professor what she wants. If she does not entertain questions, then she assuredly will not want to entertain arguments.

Here it will be instructive to illustrate what I mean by "arguing." Arguing in this sense is intellectual and never personal. Tempers do not flare. People are calm and discuss an issue from different viewpoints. There is little-to-no emotional appeal. Only the uninformed and incapable students make arguments that seek emotional appeals. Additionally, these arguments never resort to attacking the person. They only attack the main point at issue.

Arguing is an effective way of earning respect from your teacher, if done with care. Arguments most often occur in the social sciences like political science and economics. There are not a lot of your fellow students who are able to make logical and professional arguments. This is a great way to stand out from them.

The importance here is winning your professor. The importance is not winning the argument. If your teacher likes a good intellectual discourse, then give her one! Remember, you have already begun to get a feel for your professor. You can now realize just what she wants.

Be very selective and deliberate. If you sense that your professor is given to emotional appeals, then do not attempt to introduce an intellectual argument. In fact, do not argue with her at all. Be silent. Let one of your well-intentioned and intellectually curious comrades barge into the conversation and destroy their chances of getting the A grade.

Conversely, be the first to give the argument if your professor enjoys an intellectual debate. This will furthermore set you apart from your peers. Facing off with a highly educated and confident professor in front of your colleagues can be terrifying. If you are the first to speak in this instance, then you have set yourself up as a leader. Teachers are always looking for that special student in each class. The individual. The one who is creative. The leader. This tactic will allow you to satisfy this in your professor.

Additionally, there is an art to allowing the professor to win the argument without appearing weak. There are many times where you will want to allow the professor to save face in front of the class. Do this without appearing weak. Appearing weak would hurt her perception of you. Project the image that you did not consider that point of view if you must save face. Always allow your pride to take a backseat to your work on winning over the professor.

Ultimately, arguing with a professor should only be done with the strictest discretion. Use your senses. Use your judgment. Never allow your professor to feel insecure and always allow her a chance to save face. She will have the last laugh when you do not receive the A grade. It is all about the A! Always keep focused on this.

## Following Up on the Argument

A great way to cement your work on the professor is to follow up on the argument. You hardly ever need to "win" the argument, as described previously. Approach your professor in the days after the argument. Two days is a good guideline. Tell her that you have been thinking a lot about what she said. Tell her that you never thought of the issue in those terms. Keep the tone of the discussion light and friendly. Excessive sincerity or excessive flippancy will do damage to your cause, as you will look either disingenuous or unstable. Keep this encounter brief. Do not linger.

Brevity and time are two important concepts of this tactic. Brevity allows you to deliver a positive feeling in her direction. Lingering in her office will appear too sincere as if you are seeking philosophical advice.

Time is important as it shows you have had time to think about the argument. You would appear to be vulnerable or abrasive if you immediately went to them after the class and attempted this technique. You would not want to wait two weeks to approach them either. You would seem very strange. Keep it light.

Two days is a good benchmark, as it shows it's been on your mind and her words are important to you and are affecting you in a meaningful way. Ahh, vanity again. Use this to your advantage. The words and thoughts that make a professor feel most important!

## Dress and Appearance: Unconscious Attacks on the Competition

Your appearance presents a message. Your competitors' and professors' dress also send messages. Be sensitive to all of these nonverbal messages. Awareness of these messages involving dress allows you to stand out from your peers as much as help you read the professor.

## Other Students' Dress

It is the norm in a lot of college classes for students to attend class in what they wore to bed the night before. This sends a message to others, and especially to the professor, that the student does not view the class as serious. Would you show up to a wedding in a T-shirt or buy life insurance from a person in pajamas? Of course not. Your dress sends a clear message to everyone about your priorities.

Dress neatly. This does not mean you have to put on a three-piece suit or a tuxedo. Blend in without blending in. Do not totally out dress your contemporaries; just take it up a couple notches. Wear a collared shirt and jeans if your friends are wearing pajamas and athletic clothes to class. Wear a buttoned down shirt if your colleagues' norm is wearing collared shirts. Subtlety in this escalation is important.

Never look like a peacock. Dressing like a peacock will do three things: First, it will alienate you completely from the other students. This will magnify any jealousy that they may have already. Second, it will draw unnecessary attention from your professor. You will look completely artificial and any effort to "win the professor" will be hindered. Finally, it will expose your deliberateness to other students. Subtlety in dress is key. Gradually take the level up in manner of dress.

## Your Professor's Dress

Observe carefully how your teacher dresses. Do not show up in a stiff suit if she is a free spirit. Do not show up with a tie-dyed T-shirt if your professor is buttoned down and straight laced.

Do not totally mimic your professor's dress. Keep in mind also how the other students are dressed. Mirror your professor's dress as subtly and casually as you are able. You are sending the message to her that you are like her. Remember that getting the A grade will greatly hinge on factors deriving from your professor's sense of self and sense of you.

You can establish a common bond through this nonverbal form of communication. It is a very effective way of sending the professor the message: "I am like you when you were my age." Such sympathies and feelings will combine with the full gamut of other nonverbal messages you are sending. They will all culminate to help your professor identify with you, remember you, and make up her mind about giving you the A grade.

Having a well-groomed appearance that is just a couple notches above your pajama-clad competitors will be an effective tool. You will send the message to your professor that you considered her class important enough to look presentable. You will also communicate a tangible and distinguishable difference between yourself and the competition. You can also play on the professor's sense of self and identify with them.

## Review Process of Your Papers: Establish a Rapport with Instructors

It is time to "work on the professor" after you have painstakingly reviewed your own writing. As previously mentioned, your professor is the sole authority and will give you whatever grade they want. Demonstrate a propensity for hard work to them. Make them feel important. The following will discuss how to win your professor through writing papers.

Begin a conversation with your professor immediately when the course begins and carry it on throughout the semester. The best way to this is through the paper-writing process.

Take your draft (which you have already reviewed at least twice) to her at least three weeks in advance. First, this will shock and impress her. She is seasoned in her experience in dealing with students year after year. She is used to a majority of these students rushing in and out of her office abruptly a few days before the deadline. Breaking the rhythm from other students will be a pleasant surprise to her. She will automatically be inclined to assume good things about you.

Second, your professor will always suggest improvements to the writing. Put them on your paper! Make the revisions regardless of their accuracy. She is the sole audience and the sole grader. Remember, give them a little whisky...

Your professor wants to see her suggestions reflected in your paper for two reasons: First, professors like to see that their students are learning. Making the revisions shows that you are absorbing what she's been teaching all along. Most professors are writers themselves and they view the entire writing process as special and want you to learn it. This gives them a tangible reward.

Second, she wants to feel important and grapples with insecurities (like all other people). A writer herself, she does not want to be surpassed. She will want to assert her worthiness through the revisions to your paper. Play the game. Even if you know you have written a masterpiece, put all of her revisions in. Whether she is harboring insecurities or not, operate as if she is.

These meetings should always be done in secret. The best place is to meet with professors after class hours in their offices. Most students are playing intramural sports or napping in the afternoons. This will allow you to become familiar with the office, and she will be familiar with you being there. She sees the meetings as her instructing you and making you a better scholar (which in reality she is), but you see them as valuable face time with the instructor.

Face time is very important. After she hands back your paper with revisions, it is time to write! Follow her suggestions to the letter. Here, it is easiest to omit paragraphs or sentences that she underlined or is confused about. Recall from class the things she emphasized most. Put those ideas in your paper. Most instructors will only want to review your paper once. If your paper is really bad, then you may have to go back more frequently. Going back and implementing her suggestions will enhance your reputation with her and will make her feel very positive about the encounter.

Like all plans and tactics in war, simplicity is efficiency. Remember that you will most likely have that same professor again if she is associated with your major. If so, this extra work will pay you back twofold in enhancing your reputation as a stellar student in the future semesters.

Remember to not allow your competitors to realize what you are doing. Most of your work to get "A"s will be done behind the scenes. There is no reason at all to inform your competition about any of this. If you do, be very certain that you will deal with resentment and sabotage.

## Exam-Studying Process

Another great opportunity to win the professor is through the exam-studying process. This is another opportunity to continue the rapport with your professor throughout the semester. You have already made tremendous strides in winning the professor through the paper-writing process. Do not stop there.

Some exams are short answer, and some tests are essays or a combination of both. Your professor will provide a study guide two weeks out (generally). Work through and answer all parts immediately upon receipt of the study guide. It would usually take me around five hours to complete a study guide for history classes. This is cumbersome, but it is necessary.

Write your answers down on a separate sheet neatly. Wait a few days to avoid appearing like a sycophant. Around three days later, take it to the professor for advice. In your appointment with the professor, say something to the effect of, "I've been studying for the test coming up, and I wanted to make sure that I am on track...I've come up with a few study notes, if you wouldn't mind looking them over." Inevitably, she will be more than glad to look them over. Like in the paper-writing process, this seemingly simple action speaks volumes to your character as a student. It shows clearly that a) you care much about the class, b) you value her input, and c) you have the wherewithal to study in advance.

In this encounter, the professor will stop just short of handing you the test itself. She will write out key words and ideas that she is expecting to see on the test on your notes. This is mission-critical information. At this point, not only have you procured the very answers from the test, but you have begun studying for the test. However, the greatest importance here is that you will have continued that invaluable rapport with the professor. You can count on it that none, or very few, of your colleagues will have this tremendous advantage to count on test day.

## Displays of Virtue

There are many ways to give your professor the impression that you are a serious student, striving for success—all through appearances. Remember Benjamin Franklin as a young man? One way is to be seen studying by her, and the other is through your conduct during class.

## Critical Terrain: Fields of Fire

It is the duty of a military leader to cover every enemy avenue of approach with fields of fire coverage in a fighting position. Discern what key avenues of approach your professors are making in the halls and walkways of your university.

Identify these places. Be seen at these locations reading and outlining. Certain finesse is needed here. Never "overdo it," as you have already spent extended periods with the professor through studying and writing papers. Once a week is a good guideline. Use your discretion.

If your professor stops in a break area for a cigarette before classes, be there on a bench reading and underlining. Never do this on the day of a test, however. Every other average student will be. This tactic will have no effect on test day.

The overall idea is standing out from other students. Your professor will be impressed that you are actually reading the material when you could be playing intramural sports or getting a case of beer. Leave it there; this is not the place to approach the teacher. You want to look like you are very focused on your material in such a way that she would be embarrassed to interrupt your thoughts. Once she is gone, you can leave too. You will have achieved the desired effect.

## Communications

Subtle messages come in many forms other than dress and appearance. These are forms of communication with your professor on an unconscious level. Use everything, even your textbook.

Earlier in the handbook, I advised you to underline certain key phrases in your texts when you are studying. This is greatly beneficial while writing papers or studying for an examination. However, the primary reason to do it is because it is another opportunity to "work on the professor." Your professor will always give a reading assignment for the next class period. She will likely assume that most students have not read a word of it.

As your professor drifts around the room and instructs, she will be watching. Have your textbook open in plain sight with your richly highlighted and underlined text in full view. I always used bright, orange gel highlighters and rich, blue inks to underline. These colors are sure to stand out from the opaque color of the desk and catch the professor's eye.

This is a favorite technique of mine, as it requires no attention to be brought to you. This passive technique is proof that you read your material and that you care. This tactic is not used in auditorium style classes. It works best in small classes.

## Steady Your Aim

Soldiers are trained to breathe, focus on the target, and squeeze the trigger. They are taught to do this in the face of mounting chaos and in the fog of war. The round will inevitably miss the mark if the marksman jerks, rather than squeezes, the trigger. Do not get lost in the chaos of the class, relax and focus on your goal.

A second great display of virtue is to be seen reviewing your notes as the professor enters the class. The beginning of a class period is a moment of chaos. A lot of times the class is in an uproar of people chattering. This is not a warm reception for a professor to walk into every day. You are keenly aware and conscious of these underlying realities of moods and the teacher's feelings.

When the teacher walks in, be reviewing the notes from the previous class (with your highlighted textbook open, of course). This daily contrast will be forged in her mind. You will be astutely and peacefully studying, while the class is in disarray.

## Note Taking

Another display of virtue is note taking. On the one hand, good note taking is a traditional academic prerequisite for high grades. On the other, it is another way to work on the professor.

You understand how taxing it is to endure an uninterested audience if you have ever spoken in public. You also understand how encouraging it is if those in the audience are hanging on every word. Tactfully writing notes encourages your professor and enforces her positive view of you (the interested listener).

Artfully combining eye contact with note taking is another silent and passive way to work on your professor. Balance eye contact with the scribbling of notes. This balance is important because if you are too busy writing notes, rather than actively listening to the professor, then you become merely another disinterested person in the audience. Eye contact is the clearest indicator that a person is listening to you.

It is important to make a person feel important, heard, and understood. The greatest respect you can give is to listen actively. Notes balanced with eye contact are the primary means of achieving this effect.

## Class Attendance

Class attendance is the final portion in displays of virtue. Strive for near-perfect attendance. This is very important because it sends an explicit message to your professor and allows you to stand out from your peers. Your peers have no idea how often you go to class. They only see you when they are there. The only person recording your attendance is your professor. Attendance is another way in which you will stand out from your competitors.

Critical classes to attend are Friday classes and classes before a long break. These are the times when attendance is lowest. The low turnout maximizes this tactic's effects.

A scenario would be instructive. It is a Friday class. The other few students come late, talking as the teacher comes in and wearing pajamas. You are quietly flipping through your notes as the professor arrives. You came with a well-groomed appearance. You have your underlined and highlighted textbook placed prominently before you. You are taking notes and making eye contact with your professor and the whole class. All of these unspoken interactions create a very real message to your professor.

The rapport you have already started with your professor, in conjunction with these interactions, will secure your chances for the A grade. You will have begun to blend in without your intentions being sabotaged. You will get the A at all costs and have learned to use non-verbal communication to illustrate and compound your perceived virtue.

## Mass and Economy of Force

A commander must economize your force in one area in order to mass forces on the main objective in a military operation. For instance, the commander must pull troops from one area in order to array forces in a strong point in another area. This is a form of prioritization in military science.

Your chief resource as a student is your time. You must economize study time for a less pressing class in order to mass study time on a more pressing class.

Never spread your forces too thin. Learn how and when to concentrate your forces in the most effective ways. You will never be able to study everything at once. This prioritization will be a defense against feeling overwhelmed. Massing and economizing will be gain importance as the workloads increase thorough the semester.

## Always Reflect Positivity

Always exude positivity. The goal of exuding positivity is to elicit similar feelings in your professor when you encounter her. No one likes to feel negative, bad, remorseful, dreaded, and so forth. Everyone likes to feel positive, happy, and good about themselves. Do this even if you are depressed, having a bad day or are actually sad.

People naturally gravitate to positive people. It is a natural reflex to do so. Respond "Excellent!" when someone asks how you are doing, albeit professor or teacher. "Excellent" is not a magical word. You choose what feels right to you. You are correct in this as long as you are exuding confidence and making others feel positive.

The goal here has a key secondary effect on your competition. Other students are a myriad of motives, goals, insecurities, successes, and failures. You never know what you are encountering or how someone may be sabotaging you. An excellent barrier to any of this is a happy demeanor. It reflects confidence. It can divert those who prey on weaknesses and who have become excellent at honing in on them.

Additionally, if someone is out to discourage you, for whatever reason, it will be much harder for him or her to do so if you have had positive encounters with them. This is by no means foolproof. It is yet another dynamic to consider when dealing with the professor and your competition.

First, you reflect positivity to your professor. They will naturally be responsive to this and enjoy your company. Whether or not they realize this consciously is irrelevant.

## Remembering Your Professors are People Too

Your professors are just as human as you are. They have lives and families outside of class. We will discuss three areas in this section: wasting her time, assessing her hobbies, and flirting with her. A majority of the text has encouraged you to work on the professor with class-related means. This section will instruct you on extracurricular means.

## Wasting the Professor's Time

Your professor clocks in to work and clocks out at the end of the day. By the end of the day, she is tired and ready to break from the day's work. Never interrupt her schedule. You have already picked up a feel for your professor and have conducted pertinent surveillance and reconnaissance. The profile you have created for her includes her daily routine.

Do not seek your professor for any purpose after 4:30 p.m. if your teacher normally leaves at 5:00 p.m. sharp every day. Similarly, do not interfere with her lunch breaks, coffee breaks, or personal study times. When you do this, you are directly interfering with her personal time. Only use posted office hours, which you can find on the syllabus. If you repeatedly claim non-office time, you will become a burden. Moreover, this behavior will show disregard for the office hours posted on the syllabus.

## Call Your Professor Outside of Office Hours

Do not call your professor at home or during off-duty hours. Most people do not enjoy entertaining work-related phone calls when they are at home. Do not call even if an instructor gives you her home phone number. When you do you send the messages, or some combination of, that: 1) you have no consideration for her time; 2) you are desperate and unprepared; and 3) you did not care to ask these questions during class. A few of your desperate counterparts will be doing this. When they do it and you do not, it makes you stand out even more.

## Assessing Hobbies and Interests Outside of Academia

You will pick up on what the interests and hobbies of your professor are if you pay attention. Hone in on these. Use them to your advantage. You can pick up on these through talking with other students or hearing them from stories given in class.

An example would be instructive here. You hear Dr. Bing talking to another professor in the department office area about fishing and boating. You then find a boating magazine and read it in those high traffic areas that your teacher frequents. Remember only two or three facts about that topic. Be prepared to discuss what you like about boating if asked. Ideally, you will begin to talk about boats with the professor. Let her do the talking. You do not have to know much about boating at all. Just allow them to talk and feel good about the encounter.

## Support Staff as Key Target: Additional Measures to Maintain Success

Support staffs are an effective way to maintain your success in winning the professor. Support staff includes those at your university who often do the most work but are often ignored. These personnel include custodians, cooks, librarians, and office secretaries.

A key trait in a successful student is to observe what the crowd is doing, and do the opposite. Most of your competition will not look at these people and will largely leave these key assets unnoticed. This is great for you, because you will be resourceful and use all assets to your advantage.

## Janitors and Cooks

Custodians and cooks are the people working for a menial salary and do all of the legwork for the university. They maintain the university infrastructure.

Start a rapport with these people. Maintain a rapport with these individuals. Others, most importantly your professors, will pass by and notice you conversing with the support personnel.

This is important because it will speak volumes to your character. It will: a) show the professor that you are unlike most students, b) demonstrate your sense of decency, and c) convince professors of your genuineness as you are kind with all of the university ranks.

## Librarians

Librarians are a wealth of knowledge. You will learn a great deal from librarians in even the briefest encounters. Librarians are usually far more intelligent and worldly than the pay grade that is assigned to them by a university.

Librarians are key targets because of the logistical supply they can provide you. General Omar Bradley once said, "Amateurs study tactics, professionals study logistics." In war, the exciting part of the planning is the "execution" phase of planning (third paragraph of the Military Operations Order). The more arduous, but most critical, portion of the planning is the service and support (fourth paragraph of the Military Operations Order).

Treat the librarians as part of your overall support apparatus. The importance of writing papers in winning the professor has been expressed previously in this book. Your local librarian can overwhelmingly increase the odds of your success in the early stages of gathering research.

Approach the librarian with questions. Just as when you are in a classroom, demonstrate genuine interest and intellectual curiosity with them. Begin a rapport with your librarians. When it is time to write a paper, you will reap the benefits.

It is time to gather resources and research as soon as a topic is assigned in class. Approach the librarian and ask her about the subject in general terms. Ask where you can find good information on the subject.

The librarian is almost always very eager to help you in your search. She will give you ample and relevant sources that you will use in your paper. At the very least, she will explain the topic more thoroughly to you.

You have freed up a significant amount of time in the early stages of the paper. This allows you to economize your force in order to concentrate on another academic concern. Librarians are the gold standard of information and can be an invaluable asset in accumulating resources for assignments and research papers.

## Office Secretaries

Office secretaries are important support staff. They work in very close proximity to your professors. You will need to garner their good graces.

These people do most of the legwork for the department without the glamour of the title "professor." Their roles, in this way, are similar to the janitors and cooks.

Be the one who recognizes them and gives them credit. Begin a conversation with these people. Invest time into them. Begin as early as possible in the semester or as early as possible when you arrive at the university.

Ask the assistants questions about the university academic catalogue and classes offered. Listen to them. Listen to them for as long as they want to talk. Similar to librarians, these people are yearning to teach students about what they know but do not always get the opportunity because the average college student ignores them. Be the one of a few students who does not ignore them. You have goals, and you will use all of your available assets to attain those goals.

The assistants can provide "insider" information on scholarships that no one has applied for yet. These scholarships are hidden gems. Aside from the ability to add another scholarship award to your academic résumé, you can also receive cash!

Additionally, your professors talk to these people often. The better the impression you make on the office assistants, the more likely they are to "talk you up" to your professors. You will receive volumes of credibility from your professor when she hears how virtuous and considerate you are from these third-party insiders.

Write the assistants a thank-you card. The good use of sending this card will ensure that you have garnered their important friendship. A thank-you card will spread like wildfire among the staff. He or she will surely show it to others out of pride, appreciation, and surprise.

However, make sure the notes are sent at staggered intervals for each individual. A thank-you card looks like this:

"Dear Mrs. Tulane,
Thank you so much for what you do. I would be lost without your guidance and good advice. I am so glad you recommended me to the class [fill in blank with something specific]. I've learned a great deal and have narrowed down a lot of my courses for my major. Your hard work has not gone unnoticed. Thank you again!"

Keep it short. Include the word *you* often. This appeals to her sense of self. Also, point out something specific that she did for you. This is important because it will make the letter much more personal and have more effect. The letter will have the most personal and powerful effect if it is handwritten.

You do not exclude any of the other secretaries that you did not interface with who may be watching or nearby if you use the university mailbox rather than delivering it by hand. Mailing the note secretly and privately will establish that this is a private connection between you and her. This privacy makes the letter more intimate and increases its overall effectiveness.

The worst-case scenario from a thank-you card is five minutes of lost time. The best case is that she remembers you favorably in the following semesters, recommending you to the professors, and posting your card on the wall or her desk. They actually deserve the thanks and recognition. Remember Benjamin Franklin again? This is a very effective tool in securing the A grade and your reputation as a champion student.

Support personnel are invaluable assets. Janitors, librarians, cooks, secretaries, and all others similarly situated are good assets to your overall academic goals. Fortunately for you, most other students overlook these valuable assets. Leave no stone unturned and do not overlook any person at your university. Everyone can help you make A grade.

# CHAPTER 7:

# REINFORCING YOUR SUCCESS

**"Opportunities multiply as they are seized."**

**-Sun Tzu**

By this time you have cemented the A grade. Reinforce your success. You cannot be certain when you may return to the university for graduate school, seek advice in your field, or want a letter of recommendation.

The most effective way to reinforce your success is through handwritten thank-you and electronic notes. We touched on this in the previous chapter. In this chapter we will first look at the handwritten notes and then go on to electronic notes. We will finally discuss post college visits and contacts rosters.

## Handwritten Notes

A handwritten note has a lot of power. First, it is entirely personal. The receiver can actually see the sender's individual style through the handwriting. Additionally, it demonstrates that the sender cared enough to spend the time in doing so.

Second, it reflects good manners. As our society grows more digitally inclined, handwritten letters are actually gaining in power and effectiveness. Your competition will send a snap e-mail at the end of the semester, if at all. You, however, will reinforce all of the success you have created throughout the semester by standing out yet again. You will be the only one who took the time out of a busy day to write a letter of thanks.

## Electronic Notes

Write or call your professors at least once a year after you graduate. She will be thrilled to continue this relationship as you have made an important impression on her during your time in her class.

Use her university e-mail address. Seeing your name line in her e-mail university inbox will connect to memories she had of you in her class. This is a form of association.. Allow her to take part in the fact that you are now a young professional. If you are fortunate, the professor will continue to mentor and shape you as you go into this new life.

## Follow-Up Visits

Follow up with office visits over the years after college. It will beneficial to you, if are in the general area, to do so. Maintaining contacts over a span of years is important in any field or any endeavor you pursue. You should now build on your relationships with your professors and add them to your network.

Some preparation would be advised for such visits. Be sure to have read or viewed, at least superficially, the national news headlines. Be prepared to offer an opinion. This reinforces the image of you as the consummate student in your professor's mind. It stands in contrast to the quintessentially flippant twenty-something.

Contact and intimacy increase with the frequency of face-to-face encounters. All of your professors are professionals in their fields. Most of your professors can continue to offer valuable insights and unique ideas that will benefit you in your field. Some of your professors are highly respected authorities in their fields. The benefits of a continued and years-long relationship with them are boundless.

## Contact Rosters

Create a contact roster. It is hard to be young in any profession. The more people you have relationships with, the more frequently opportunities arise.

I have kept two books since college. One address book contains all of my college contacts. The other contains all of my military contacts. I write the person's name at the top. I also record all information, such as mail addresses and phone numbers. Finally, I record unique information about that person. I record the name of his or her spouse, names of his or her children, and one or two words about his or her interests.

Social sites are incredible for networking. Look through your friends' lists from time to time. Look for those individuals from your university whom you have not contacted in a while, especially one of your professors. Leave a message and always include a piece of that personal information from your file on her.

Compile lists of contact information from your professors and fellow students. Your fellows are no longer your academic competition. Now they are colleagues. Many of your colleagues will become highly successful. Your professors will continue to remain in their positions and/or advance as well. You may benefit from others' successes only if you are remembered.

## Who Will Remember You?

Being remembered by your professors in the years to come will be an extra benefit. This is outside of making the A grade. All people are valuable and important as contacts. Do not throw away the success you have made for yourself. Continue to draw resources from your college experience. A contact roster is the most effective way of networking and reinforcing your success from college.

# CONCLUSIONS

"The different measures suited to the nine varieties of ground; the expediency of aggressive or defensive tactics; and the fundamental laws of human nature: these are the things that must most certainly be studied."

**-Sun Tzu**

You now can take ownership of your academic future. Sun Tzu breaks terrain down into nine categories. He analyzes the offense and the defense. For academics, he draws from human nature. Sun Tzu and Machiavelli are relevant to this day because they offer valuable insight into the unchanging human nature. This nature remains constant in the face of technology, globalization, and centuries. All of us are at times susceptible to greed, arrogance, joy, anxiety, and excitement. Learning to identify these in others will allow you to use this nature to your advantage.

Human nature is as dark as the power artists who manipulate it. Our literary and spiritual histories express this common theme throughout all the ages. Do not be one of the sheep.

Use them to be aware of those who are constantly manipulating events to their favor. A good understanding of these dynamics that are usually entirely on the unconscious level will help you fend off the salesman attempting to rob you, the co-worker attempting to deceive you, or the political leader attempting to lie to you.

Combine these interpersonal tactics with diligent study. Studying alone will produce results. However, the tactics herein will provide you with a decided advantage over your competition if exercised alongside diligent study.

I encourage you to take these principles and build on them. Never stop observing. Never stop reading. Develop your own techniques and procedures. This has been an overview of my experiences in making the A grade. Seize and hold academic success now that you have a better understanding of all the dynamics going on beyond the classes, exams, papers, and studying.

# Appendix A: Nine Principles of War (US Army)

**Mass**: Concentrate combat power at the decisive place and time.

**Objective**: Direct every military operation toward a clearly defined, decisive, and attainable objective.

**Offense**: Seize, retain, and exploit the initiative.

**Surprise**: Strike the enemy at a time, at a place, or in a manner for which he is unprepared.

**Economy of force**: Assign minimum essential combat power to secondary efforts.

**Maneuver**: Place the enemy in a position of disadvantage through the flexible application of combat power.

**Unity of command:** For every objective, ensure unity of effort under one responsible commander.

**Security:** Never permit the enemy to acquire an unexpected advantage.

**Simplicity:** Prepare clear, uncomplicated plans and clear, concise orders to ensure thorough understanding.

## Appendix B: Selected Reading List

*The Prince* by Niccolo Machiavelli

*The Autobiography of Benjamin Franklin* by Benjamin Franklin

*On War* by Carl Von Clausewitz

*The Art of War* by Sun Tzu

*US Army Field Manual 3-0 (Operations)*